To Hold Awhile

To Hold Awhile

Ron Atkinson

Limen Books

QUALICUM BEACH • BRITISH COLUMBIA

1997

Canadian Cataloguing in Publication Data

Atkinson, Ron, 1933-
To hold awhile

ISBN 0-9682315-0-0

1. Title.
PS8551.T56T62 1997 C818'.54 C97-910536-6
PR9199.3.A787T62 1997

Published by
LIMEN BOOKS
Box 21, Qualicum Beach
BC V9K 1S7 Canada

Printed and bound in Canada by
MORRISS PRINTING COMPANY LTD.
Victoria, British Columbia

for

DONNA

with my love

The author wishes to express his gratitude
to the artist KEN FLETT
for the photo on the front cover
of his mixed-media on silver-print painting
Dancing with Shadows

with thanks to
DONNA *and* KEN
and the
KILGOURS

reproductions of watercolours
and pen and ink sketches
including self-portraits from boy to man
are by the author

Let it Be as the Wind

If silence be broken, let it be as the wind, moving branch on branch. If the slow hush be disturbed, let it be as a loon paddling the calm sea. If words be spoken, let them be as blue grapes hidden among green leaves. If thoughts be bared, let them be as love's body is bared in the warm sun. If names be given, let them be as the light through gull's wings. If prayers be prayed, let them be as breathing when it is most easy. If any god be sought, let it be the incarnate one, whose dwelling this world is.

Contemplation by Canoe

Again, in the old canoe, slide out from sun-warm rocks to find the pulse of paddle and sea.

Go far out to centre where the encircling mountains are reflected dark, white and blue. Lay the paddle down, yourself down too.

Outstretched and open, yield to the whole air, the sea and sky. Let the craft drift, rock with the rip, turn with the tide, flow with the current. Enfolded in mountains, a gathering edge of cumulus and snow-scented winds, let yourself enjoy a more kindly breathing. With eyes closed, let the slow, unfathomed turning float and free you.

Here is your oldest kin, here is your true belonging, your largest and last self in a time that is timeless.

Physical Joy

We are rich. We live in the physical world. We abandon ourselves to the sensuality of daily life. There is always wood to be chopped, fish to be filleted, a fence to be mended. I discover an old grindstone in the cellar and sharpen an axe for the first time in my life, turning the wheel with my foot. I enjoy the heft of the handle in my hand.

A neighbour is teaching me to make my own cedar shakes and loans me his fro and mallet. The snap, as the sleek wood splits and falls away, is delicious. And I am reclaiming an old vegetable garden. When the handle of my shovel breaks, I manage to hammer in a new one, making one out of two old ones. While I turn over clods of twitch grass, a raven steals an orange peel from the compost and alights on the clothesline with it. White sheets are drying in the west-wind and the sun. When crows pester the raven, a jet black and bright orange streak gleams up into the bluest sky.

Nightwatcher

Look again nightwatcher, for the one who is coming is often the one who has come. Many Messiahs later, it would still be true, for the present is bearer of the ultimate.

This watching of the night began so long ago. The child at the window breathes an opening through the carved fronds and leaves of frost etched in the window-pane. He rubs his warm fist to melt a hole through which he may see the moon on the sculpted snow below. While the child kneels to watch, to tend the forms of things in crystal, the rose bed sleeps in the snow, the bare maple cracks in the sheath of ice.

Yet nightwatcher knows that advent adventures still in a round will to be full.

Look again. The unlikely one who is there for you now may be the one for whom you have long watched.

In Our Element

It is easier to be than we make it seem.
The world is as right for growing soul as for growing grass.
Grace is as persistent as rain, as sweet as sun.
We are turned to our truth, as surely as tides to the moon.
As all growing things seek the sun, we turn to tenderness.
We flow in our element as bird in air or fish in sea.
We are natives of the very life we awoke within.
We are already immersed in the sacred deep we seek.
Belonging to time's wholeness, there is nothing to fear.
Affirming life's energies we join life's best dream.

A Twilight Faith

Treasuring the quieter energies of evensong, I fear morning meditations may presume too much. By evening the striving ego permits a more tender resilience. Hopefully, by the end of the day a darker wisdom is possible.

Let us bring to crepuscular contemplation only those traditions which assume nothing arrogant. The holy well from which we draw is very old and very deep.

A time of reverie in twilight draws upon a shadowy belonging beyond our naming.

Sensual Roots

On my knees again, weeding, I remember that first day of permission to work in the garden. Nine years old, I was entrusted with the splitting up of iris bulbs. I knelt as any acolyte of spring. My fingers learned the pleasure of probing secrets of soil, the redolent memorial place of so many rotted lives.

So soon after the last snow patches, the heady scent of earth awakens strange stirrings.

The burls of old bulbs looked dead. Knotted and gnarled clusters, not easily parted, I had been assured lived all the better for first being broken apart.

When the dead bulbs burst into silken flags, burgundy, blue, bearded in purple velvet, I too swelled in a new way.

The earth child in us remains, dreaming still of renewing our role of husbandry in the garden.

We never outgrow the sensual roots of complicity and longing.

Evensong

The Kwakiutl elders hold a weekly meeting in the shape of a voyage, a soul journey, sailing out and back again. They sing together for an hour, share a few words of prayer, and then sing for another hour with an awesome slowness in long arcs straight as an arrow. It is the sound of luminous lamenting stretched as tight as a drumskin. It is evensong as enchantment possessed of one breath.

I take the path home by the turbulent sea under a huge sky of stars, as in a dream, while the sound of ages flows like fire in my blood.

I will call upon them to come and sing for the healing of those who are hurting or nearing the end.

In Streams of Wholeness

We honour that holy wisdom which lives by gratitude as much as desire. To silent light, fountain of joy, we offer our delight as well as our care. We let ourselves move in the flow of that light, strengthening the will in streams of wholeness. We let ourselves belong to this intimate, vast and single source of hidden springing.

We may dare dreams kindred with all that is, gently pulled along by a slender thread of imagination in the hungry body of shalom. We gather every remembrance and every hope, singing together prayers of the possible.

A Welcoming Fire

When the dry season of a summer is over, and autumn rains make it safe enough to burn garden cuttings, the town permits small fires in our yards.

Aside from delinquents whose toxic fumigations begin with tires and end with styrofoam, they recall childhood days when golden piles of fallen leaves were offered before every household. Seeds of firs and seeds of grain belong together in our story. To be human is to have a hand in burnings natural and domestic, slow photosynthesis and quick consummation.

A friend who lives on five acres in the country keeps a special burning place. Lately, he has been saving and bundling the cuttings from spring pruning, to burn respectfully, bundle by bundle.

It has happened before when he invites us to visit him at night. He has set a welcome fire. Standing with him around a burning born of care for his orchard, we gaze upon the shifting coals and embers of fiery sculpture in a sweet-scented spending.

A primal and healing joy ignites the three of us.

She Held On

The lamb slain from the foundation is no stranger, but a forgotten ancestor, a neglected neighbour.

We live so close to countless lives laid down in sacrifice. Military deaths are but a fraction of the mute and anonymous deaths which bring life to this hour. The fallen in battle especially suffer and die in the hidden strife of daily ordeal in a prevailing disorder.

It takes a host of suffering servants to sustain us all. Begin by remembering one among many. Remember one. After her children were scattered, her husband run down by a drunk driver, and her body invaded by cancer, she held on. Quietly cheerful and brave her hope for a better world was contagious.

Many still live off the grace of her strength.

The life of the world depends upon unknown upholders of a quiet hope.

The Rim of Our Desire

Between these narrow gates where the moments leap, we must suddenly choose to jump into life and live.

By a chain of little freedoms, by small risk afer small risk, we make our gradual oblation. We shape the edge of our longing, the rim of our desire, by those resinous moments hidden like pitch in the grain of a dry snag.

In the narrowness of time, an incendiary largeness holds us.

In the slight friction of minute choices, here and now, the eternal catches fire.

Snow and Roses

The roses continue in a winter so mild. They still struggle to bloom around the fishpond taking their cue from fish who refuse to bed down for the winter. When I brought in a bouquet on Christmas day, I thought it the last. In January's gentle rains the Joseph's Coat continues to climb, bearing blooms a little smaller and a shade more pale. We watch them tenderly, or rather they watch us at the window.

I prune them cautiously in hopes of giving them a rest, but they only assert themselves all the more. They are like those brave old souls who fight for dignity to the end. Who doesn't try to sneak out of life's darker seasons? Who can do nothing even in winter?

We wake to mute snow that fell in the night. The darkened pond is still limpid with bright gold fish gliding serenely within. But the tubs of blood-red roses alongside are heavy with their white burden. They haven't made it easier on themselves by staying on so long.

As we age, so much happens to make life harder. When we already fail to fill the hours, a perverse will keeps us awake to wrestle in the night as well.

Yet, we are as reluctant as roses in snow to bend down before we must.

Shore Time

We yield to the transforming will which calls forth the form of things.

As the tide takes the beach, time takes us all in its turning. After many moons, nothing is left the same on the newly scoured beach, while the sea rolls on. We are like frail sanderlings relishing the roar and crash of tumult breaking just beyond us.

On leaden, windless days we wait breathless and stranded.

On the coldest days of winter we pick passing shards of crystal from a frozen fringe of ocean.

In spring a new edge white with milt and pollen.

Never the same shore, yet the same great sea.

Sliding into Home Base

Counting the cost of chance, the expense of reality, we savour, nevertheless, a taste for living. We affirm every gift in the joy of ambiguity. For life includes death hovering in the grace of free play. In the dance of mortality, we thrive on bittersweet coincidence, vitality in opposition, peace in tension, communion in confrontation.

We are like children playing until night, mud-spattered, and breathless, sliding into home base. In grace sure as gravity, we know the fine art of balancing between our first fall and our last.

The meaning is in the gamble, while the play goes on, until it's far too late and just too dark. Yet while the rope swings in the eternal now, we jump between our first breath and our last in this sweet, slight arc of embodied dreams.

An Earlier Affirmation

I am summoned daily by birds, familiar fellow creatures: the elated eagles, their shrieking, like the whinny of wild horses; gulls choosing life as scavengers of the given; hungry wrens, tiny and comic gymnasts; the amused brown creeper, viewing life upside down; the lamenting loon who finally assents with calm liquidity. In these, I recognize myself in an earlier affirmation in feathers, when I could fly, as now in dreams I still do. I admire, I envy an almost forgotten part of our story. What seems other is also deep within, for we share a common evolving on our uncertain earth, our brief dwelling place.

Twice now I have planted grass seed where I had to remove a dying shrub. Sparrows and Towhees, come joyously several times a day to peck out the seeds. At first Teddy bounded after them imperiously but has acquiesced to my command that they be left to feed happily. He lies down at the French door of the cabin looking out at them with puzzled longing. It is a triage he does not yet understand, permission when no wrong is done to let the hunger of others prevail.

Seeing them close nourishes me, restores them to the body of my larger self, and one day I will plant again.

A Sea Change

The young man and woman are walking away hand in hand towards the rolling surf, stiff and tense, shoulders arched.

On tip toe, shuddering as the icy brine swamps their loins, they disappear into a smashing breaker.

The lusty sea plays roughly with their bodies delivering them to a salty sweep of wildness.

Coming back to shore glistening, they stand taller, stronger, walking now a little apart.

She walks with a vigorous lightness, gracefully swinging her hips. He strides with a new swagger.

They are laughing.

They stop to embrace.

Their kiss is deep and long.

Hunter Envy

I envy the proud, so very blue and blazing Kingfisher. I have glimpsed that keen eye, heard that confident cry and admired the accurate arc of that dazzling dive. How beautiful is the clarity of the swift and sure! No kingfisher begs for the beyond or confuses error with mystery. He delights only in the act of precision. He has a good stomach for the facts. Arrogance enjoys the felicity of hunger's swift action.

To be human is to permit complications queer and kind.

We can never be sure of consummations devoutly wished.

A Brief Beauty

By their sense of one another more than sixty kinglets fly as one being.

They turn and dive together to land and flutter around the fishpond, bright blurs of gold and ruby. They may be unaware of the hibernating goldfish which lie hidden in the rich protection of silt.

As they do for an hour or two every October, the kinglets feed exuberantly on fallen seeds in the flower-pots. Two or three enjoy a felicitous bath in the saucer pads of the water lilies.

Suddenly they are gone . . . and it is winter.

Intimacy of the Ultimate

We meet in hosannas of irony, hallelujahs of the unlikely, the realm of nevertheless. For reality is shy and slow to tell all. Things are not what is said and not what they seem.

We meet in koans of complexity where the slightest impulse invites the ultimate. For every day we die a little.

So we come to the rebel rabbi riding his donkey as clown king, leading the amused crowd into the arena of paradox.

The freedom of a life laid down in irony.

After

After such separate pain in the night, morning words begin over through tears without truth. So it is not yet to be, and the day is bitter, empty and long. After words as weapon, after the slammed door, the silence.

Face to face again, the unexpected collapse of definitions and defenses calls for a way deeper than words. Finally at table, a loaf of coarse bread, two cups of red wine, a white candle's flame.

Nothing for now to say, nothing to beg or implore, dread or explain. Once again, simply the sharing of daily bread and common cup.

Then the familiar bed of their embracing.

The Shyness of Being

We wait with you, tracing our dream, dark secret, looking for consolations of the sorrowful, for emblems of empathy. Gifted with emptiness, we may yet come to love the virginal veil of promise. The chaste enigma of nature enthralls those who fall into her dreams.

Descending dews, night frosts, morning mists, disappearances, diminishments, perishings, ember fires, coals of desire, benedictions, rainswept leaves, the final falling, the last chrysanthemum, the thin ice of fragile ponds, ferns and webs – the shapes of swift, diaphanous things, small and shy.

Rose petals fall on spreading crystal. An irresistible dance of veils lures us to lie down warm in the snow.

Native to this World

Life is larger and kinder than we knew. There is a wider margin for a wilder purity. The way of a generous and forgiving will places permission at the heart of our dreams.

By a fresh freedom for our every wish, yes comes quietly to abolish every no. We stand ever at the beginning in the hot flow of our native blood.

Songbirth

She awakens in the night with an aching need to sing. As often, near full moon, leaving her bed, she sits at the window by the boiling tide. She is a woman in her soul's labour, the song growing with the pain. Sometimes it takes until dawn to bring forth the sorrow, the joy, and beyond these, her womanly wholeness.

There was a time when he listened. Only once did he beg her to come to bed. "No, you must leave me alone!" Now, he can lie on his deaf ear. For it is too much for him, the keening, the wailing, until the clear stream of song flows from her.

In the morning after her songbirth she is stronger than ever, and her silence deeper.

With Descant

It is a day of remembering, an evening of memories, a night of emptying branches, blessed and bereft, beautiful and sad. We seek an equilibrium of grief and exultation. If we wait for a just world, we will go in mourning forever.

The moon is caught in the branches, clouds scuttle across the mind. We hear the dark song of anguish. Yet a descant rises over all.

No Other Emblem

Walking wet woods in a dripping stillness, suddenly a sharp tapping and steady drilling . . . a pileated woodpecker, happily hammering in search of supper. Here's a crested creature bigger than a jay in red, white and black, colours of aggressive affirmation, energies of lust, an elation despite trespasses. We need no other emblem of grace. Suddenly we sense a permission to call upon a primal pardon. We walk in creation's irrational urge towards absolution.

That life may continue to call forth life.

An Island of Rust

We found a gift at the shore, a slab of rusted iron from a ship's galley stove – a ragged, broken body full of wounds, inviting us to the fragile fullness of this brief day.

Not Only These Snowdrops

They say it is presumptuous and wasteful to venture into space. We should attend to our earth, we who have hardly settled here, who know so little of this planet, so little about how to cleanse her bloody history, her wounded body.

Yet to be human is bravely to be at the dubious edge breaking old taboos and inhibitions. It is not enough to cherish only these snowdrops at our feet. We are also to find affinity in stars; not only to be grounded under the sun, but to seek space on other ships of the universe.

And the day will come when we will both care for this crowded earth, and emigrate from her hungry shores.

Hope of room at the end demands unworldly colonizing.

We Would Live Freely

We would live humbly on this earth, in awe of all that lives, alert to the full diversity of the divine descending.

We would live wholly for this earth, in affinity with fellow creatures, belonging to the one family of the cosmic net of creation.

We would live proudly on this earth, not as strangers nor as aliens, but as natives of creation by our very birthright.

We would live closely with this earth, taking part with all in the slow drama of our evolving through the play of the one in the many.

We would live bravely on this earth, honoring the mystery in our midst and deep within us.

We would live freely on this earth for the songs of others and the very song of self, in the harmonium of all.

Laughter at Night

The three of us are sitting on the porch as the last bit of light yields to dark. I am listening to them share something of their grief. Now we sit in a heavy silence for their sorrow is truly beyond speaking. There is only the pulse of waves splashing far out at the ebbtide edge, from the wake of an invisible ship passing in the straits. They have had such a long hard life, and still new hurts come to pain them more.

At last the old man clears his throat to speak. Then gently chuckling to himself, he asks "Do you see that little bit of moon, all that is left?" There is but a slender sickle of waning moon glimmering over the other island. With his way of drawing out the vowels, he tells us, "I turn around and ask myself, how that little bit of moon will pull the tides tonight?" As is his habit, he repeats himself again and again, and every time his joke amuses him. His wife's thin, high chuckle joins in, their laughter rolling out into the night, to the stars, and the thin moon.

An In-Between Time

A calm summer evening for relaxing in a seaside pub. I sit between regulars and strangers feeling both kindred and alone.

The fishermen are stretching their stories. A man and a woman are playing darts. Note the tilt of hips and buttocks. Raunchy studs strut their stuff for a table of young women.

The ripened sun hovers beyond masts and rigging, tangled silhouettes of trollers, gillnetters, seiners and sloops. The gulls and crows, white and black in the rosy glow, shriek and croak in disgust and delight. On the far coast snowy slopes are turning gold.

A sole duck makes a limpid late dive in the dusk.

Overcast

On a memorable day of school we learned the four lovely names for the clouds. We hailed them all: wispy filaments of cirrus wooing rain, stratus riding clean on high, nimbus with her arms full of wet, and especially, cumulous piled so profusely and so white.

Meanwhile, we still wander with clouds of unknowing, as in a cosmic maze, where every secret is protected for the immense undisclosed whole. Although a cloudless blue astonishes and delights, we know the lucid and the clear can't last for long, for a day is the difference a wind makes.

We may meet as believers in the morning but must come to evening as reverent agnostics.

It's only later looking back that we remember night is as right as day, and foul weather fair in it's way.

Bread and Poetry

We sleep in dreams which nourish and enrich us. We wake in gifts of grief and gladness. Night and day utter forms of the nearby eternal. Out of gratitude, we long to gather in acts of celebration, in ceremonies of elation. We would meditate on poems of exultation. . . .

Yet, we are unworthy celebrants, for we have wounded the innocent. We have wasted and spent wantonly. We have squandered the narrow bounds of earth.

Will we treasure this world more dearly, that the gift of life may go on giving? Will we learn the particular dignity of shared bread?

The most precise compassion is a just ecology.

We await the marriage of bread and poetry.

After A Native Elder

I like the big house where we share the same smoke. Part of the winter wind, we join the one in the sky who hungers for us. Your smoke and my smoke are one in the smoke of the great burning in our midst.

The dancing and feasting must come to an end. The laughing eagle shall yield to the sobbing dove, the wolf to the family dog. Soon the ceremony of winter will be only a mound of wet ashes. We have seen the great people come and go. We have seen them turn into flickering shadows out of the embers of the fire. So much life has passed up through the smoke hole. Unremembered sparks have joined themselves to the stars. Soon we shall leave our big house for the little shelter, leave our big fire for the last trail fires.

We spend our lives like blue wisps of smoke, a fragrant incense that turns to ash. We know only a fugitive repose. Yet it is precisely this – a slight, swift fragility – which secures for us a very mortal joy.

Immersion

After a loon-still calm, something other is urged. The rain in my sleep pours forth speech. A night-turning wind southeasters my dreaming. September wakes me in a wilder light. Like the violent smashing of waves on shore, I would be taken and turned for my own dive into my essential deep. The hunger of this stormy soul exults in active immersion, baptism in the agony of the accountable world.

I would rid myself of bell, book and candle, and know the friction of facts, the passion of flesh and blood. But how will I know the incarnate life and present my body to be incorporated?

The habit of being discarnate is hard to break.

Thoughts in We-wai-kai Museum

Beyond nameless fears and denials, beyond inflationary rage, remember the rugged islands of hope, the beachheads of uncommon kindness. For after every drowning deluge, an unquenchable will ignites the art of a human welcoming. While the sway of violence threatens, the way of compassion also grows through adventures in gentleness. Remember the welcoming bonfires of native hospitality at the edge of the shore.

In Cape Mudge Village two "welcome poles," which once stood on the beach to greet visitors, now stand at the entrance of the museum which houses returned relics, treasures taken at the time the potlatch was outlawed.

Welcome to a vision that is larger than we imagined.

Between cultures, between times old and new, between persons whose truths are hidden, there is so much to misunderstand.

The Nuyumbaless Society has created a protected place of remembrance and awe.

How good it is, in this museum, to muse upon the bridge between memory and hope.

The Right Side of a Door

The country road came to a dead end at iron gates locked in a stone wall. Signs read: Private Property No Trespassing. While I have no wish to visit the stranger who shut himself in and me out, I wonder about the wisdom of making the home a castle.

We all need privacy and crave sanctuary, the richness of a chosen solitude. There is no need to apologize for the peace of a genial retreat, a haven of aloneness without loneliness.

Yet, how will we hear the knock at the door to welcome arrivals as gifts?

Fearing the intruder, we shield ourselves from threatening invasions, sending out signals of separation. Yet worse than fearing the uninvited knock is being locked in a lonely isolation. Waiting in vain for the right call – finally no longer expecting anyone to approach us at all.

We need a beautiful boundary between the self and the other, an elegant balance between solitude and society.

How sweet is the felicity of finding ourselves on the right side of the door.

Not Ourselves Alone

That we may know the word beyond words, we sink into a still listening. That we may know a truth beyond knowledge, we relax in the gift of mystery. That we may receive and be received, we trust the opening of old gates. That we may find the very body of being, we honour all that is human. That we may know what is human, we find ourselves in the continuum of creation, kindred with all.

For we are not ourselves alone. Our identity is infinite. Our health is in this wholeness, our destiny is communal, spirit and flesh one body. The cosmic multitude is the one to whom we belong.

Integrity is to find ourselves in this spectrum.

Washing Windows

I just wonder, while cleaning windows, if they ever come clean. The streaks and specks are always on the other side from the one you're on. I go inside and do a thorough job of it. No, that smear has to be outside. I put the ladder back and do my best. No, the dirt is on the inside, after all. Or is it?

Rubbing away, I think how like care of the soul is the cleaning of windows.

In the last rays of light, the smudges show up again, on the inside.

Hearth and Heart

The room glowing in firelight from dry maple is warm and soft. Tending blue and amber coals in the hearth, kindles a remembering repose. I fall back into the past, sink into a slow calm.

A vein of sap sizzles in the troubled hearth. Logs shift, a crack opens, hissing sparks leap from the grate. Removing a tiny meteor jars me out of my quiet. An old restlessness wedges open a crack in my reverie.

For there is another burning where the domestic hearth fights the longing heart.

I go to the window where bare branches of the peach tree flutter and scrape. The wind is rising. A dog barks from across the ravine. I press against the dark. I am looking out – for what? There is nothing, no one, not yet.

The hungry fire is ready for another armful of maple wood.

Song of Songs

All songs sing one song, all stories tell one story: the terrible wonder of I and Thou, dangerous adventures in eros, experiments in search of the single body of love.

For we are the sacrament of one another. It is not our doing but freedom's seminal desire in the fields of grace where we met and meet.

Creation calls us to her covenant.

Poised between birth and death, entrusted with all mysteries, girded with the towel of tenderness, we would empty our egos, align with destiny, in the freedom of life before death.

We are invited to sing, with the Song of Songs, of love that is stronger than death.

Genial Font

When womb opened to world, we were held so close, rocked at the breast, song flowing with milk. We learned to cry, to kick, to choose. We joined the others, asserting our selves. Seeing her smile, we smiled back. Hearing her words, we found our voice.

Yes, from the woman in whom we first moved, we learned that life may be trusted.

This must be the beauty which compels us now, and all our days, and at our ending.

The Haven of Now

There are so many goodbyes. We are always having to let go of those on earth we loved. Lonely and empty, we wait for them to walk through the door. We wonder how there can be so much to accept. We are appalled to find death so commonplace, too early, too extravagant – victims of terror and error, innocent lives laid down in a daily and dubious battle.

In angry or bewildered grief, we become slow to turn to the gift of another, to open and let in new love. We desperately need the courage of trust, the strength to say yes and begin again. For, however beautiful the past, only the present is holy.

There is no peace but an adventurous one in the reckless haven of now.

Original Whimsy

Are we hugely repressed, smothering our mortal happiness? Do we merely imitate each other, cultivating a grave sobriety? Do we wear a mask to masquerade among the mature? This world is such a serious place on an earth heavy with debts. There are so many threats to remembered innocence and the impossible makes every demand upon us. Only the smallest muffled voice hints at another and lighter way. The sacred muse of amusements invites us to yield to the original whimsy, the joke which must have blessed the beginning.

If only we were no longer so fiercely in charge here, but glad to play a playful part. If only we knew about growing up by growing down to earth in an embracing ease where all is right enough for now, with a roundness coming, staying and going.

In birth, life and death, we are invited to embody love's triad in her true cycling.

Entanglement

There is a jealous force that throws an invisible net over love's embracing, and laughs at sleeping lovers entrapped in their enchantment. Even the most pure hunger is laced with lust in this net of opposing wills.

In the great sea, we sink all the lures of love, "the devices and desires of the heart" only to find that we ourselves are prisoners of erotic beauty caught and bound by the fisher king.

Yet we would love widely and deeply despite the entangling net thrown over every quest for communion.

Die Laughing

He is trying to weed the garden, but can no longer control his limbs, his arms flaying about in awkward, futile jerks. He crawls to me on his hands and knees, and stares up at me with an absurdly happy face. He has me help him into a garden swing where we sit together.

Conversation by now is impossible. Yet he seems to have something beautiful to tell me. He searches my eyes. Do I understand?

Over and over, his laughter fills the garden. With a full heart, and close to tears, I can't help but join him.

At the memorial service and the wake we carry out his wish that there be no grieving or religion. It is a festive time reflecting his flamboyant Irish life. Among us, a young woman wanders, mournfully complaining that she just can't accept such hilarity.

I think of the father of a friend who died while reading an amusing book by P. G. Wodehouse. It was found open in his hand. At his memorial we read where he had left off.

"What a queer thing life is, when you come to think about it, it's quite unlike anything else."

Under the Sign of Sumac

My neighbour asks me: "Do you really want those ragged sumac on our boundary line?" He says they make a mess and would see them down, but I declare myself firmly in their favour.

Such furry, twisting limbs and "palm leaves" once hid a boy who lived in tropical story. Until the pull of this wind and rain, they proclaimed a fiery passion swelling in ripe torches of seed, blood-red with desire for the spilling.

Crouched under them, so they will give no further offense, I rake away from both our lawns any sign of their prodigal spending.

An aging man out of shape, colour and wildness needs all his emblems of lost extravangance, as he needs his unsensible friends, the sensual, free and flamboyant.

The Poem that is a Person

"Are you the one who has come or shall we look for another?"

We don't look at each other very closely, or hardly at all. To gaze upon each other is impolite. If we do permit ourselves to really see a nearby person, we are likely to be overwhelmed by the articulation of soul in body. To observe another's way of standing, walking, or just nodding, touches us tenderly. The character of the hips, personality in the wrists, grace of a wisp of hair at the nape of the neck. If the gaze is returned, we may witness the profound and precise light in the eyes of another.

I know that there is nothing so rare, nothing so unique as the person before me. Here is life's ultimate. Seekers of the holy need look no further than the naked, human poem of the person.

The divine voice affirms the one rising up from the waters, an island of human soul rising out of the sea of creation, no longer immersed in nature, but risking personality.

"This is my beloved in whom I am well pleased."

Hungry for Revelation

An exhibition of sculpture includes live persons exhibited in air-conditioned cubes of plexiglass. Utterly naked men and women pose amid sculpted nudes of stone and bronze. While most visitors pause rather briefly before these living statues, one elderly woman spends most of a morning contemplating male nudes from all angles.

A curious attendant approaches the gallery visitor as she again makes her way around a splendidly bare man.

"No doubt you're wondering why I'm staying on so long. I'm a spinster, and although an old woman now, I've never seen a naked man. I'd like to take a look before I die."

Shyly she covers her mouth with her hand but cannot repress a laugh.

"I can die happy, now."

Where Two or Three

To be human is to wonder. The circumference of ignorance grows with the radius of knowledge. For knowledge can only deepen mystery, not as perplexity, but as the mystery of the known.

In the same way, the more we know a person, the more mysterious that person becomes to us.

For each person is infinite.

Among two or three trusted friends, everything depends upon respect for the mystery which grows in their midst.

They Lead Him Away

As I open the door to leave, he steps in. We are strangers thrust suddenly so close that our eyes must meet, almost intimately. Then I see the handcuffs, see also the leg chains.

He is a young native. The swift tumult of our meeting is painfully tender. What does he expect of me? What can I be for him? He holds me by his hurting eyes, his scarred nobility.

His guards have been watching us. Abruptly they prod him on. They lead him away. His energy leaks from me, leaving me bereft.

For I have recognized him.

The man of sorrows.

The Oldest Choice in Story

They walk hand in hand between two waters on the dark path of the narrow spit, in fallen and falling leaves. They are so young. She is fair; he is strong. Above the roar of the west wind, eagles cry, raucous crows caw from old-growth firs.

At a choice of paths, the lovers take the one by which they disappear into the thickest stand of forest. Only a few red berries cling late to the huckleberry bush of yellow leaves and bronze. Bare of blossoms now, beautiful also in seed, the wild rosehips declare themselves in orange-red orbs of promise. In this secluded grove so near the white crash of breakers, the lovers linger sharing their most secret and closest selves. The narrow way trembles for the time being with every touch of their seeking and finding bodies.

Brief the wild rose, brief also the berry, on the slight earth between the wide seas.

Wide is the wonder, sweet the way when lovers brand each other with the love that chooses them.

Plots and Fences

Once again I long to be released, sprung free of the prison of this armoured ego. No longer my own meaning, I must be found in a larger one, the grace of the whole. Yet I fear becoming trapped in social contracts beyond either need or desire. I hesitate to reach out.

Who knows the art of bonds without bondage?

Light enough to be lifted up for a comic view from a height beyond the doubtful race far below, I take delight in seeing the lakes and rivers, creeks and ponds, reservoirs, churches, and especially the streets laid out in their genial pattern, the precise plots and fences of neighbourly habitation.

How endearing is society ordered for the happiness of both our coming together and our drawing apart. Suddenly, I am touched with gratitude for the shape of this simple and common privilege.

Society must breathe both in and out.

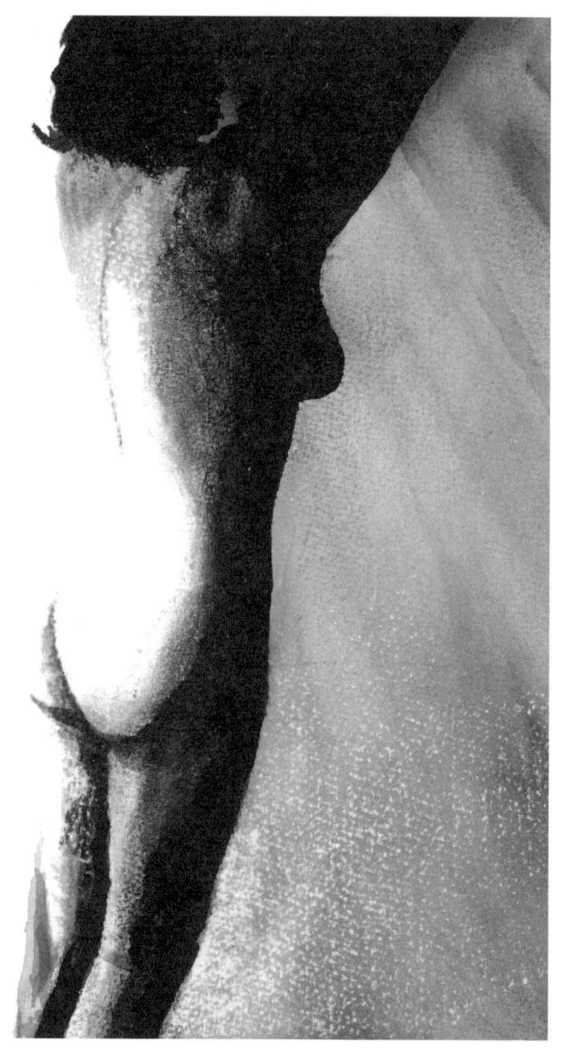

The Naked and the Clothed

It stormed all night. Snow has been falling all day. No knock at the door, no ringing phone. A time for staying inside and being kind to themselves. So they keep the fire fed by blocks of fir and alder. They linger over lunch, listening to the wind.

Somehow they take to cleaning trunks, sorting rummage from garbage. They hold up memories in fabric, the shape and scent of the past clinging to old clothes. What to keep and what to throw away while so much goes unnoticed? They ask each other, why try to swagger in fumbling fashions? Why dress at all to hide the radiance of the body?

How odd that the true blaze of the body, the face, is all that goes public. The most revealing part of us is left so unmercifully, utterly bare, the eyes finally telling all.

Meanwhile they bundle up a bag for the spring rummage sale. Someone may use their old clothes to hide the shy beauty of a spirit which only flesh articulates.

Expect no more than a glimpse of naked truth.

Refractions

Sunlight pours down on a basket of yellow apples, on tomatoes in a windowsill, on a crusty loaf of bread . . . and with familiar trembling light falls on a white cup of black tea on the blue table cloth, touching and turning one who watches towards lightness.

The slight transcendence of light on chipped china, everyday faded teacups, rinses and cleanses the hurt, eases for now the void.

Drenched in full sunlight, sharing bread, tea and tomatoes, it is hard to doubt a luminous body of hope.

His Exuberance

He never tires of convincing me that I can do things. He even takes the false mystique out of carpentry and delivers me to its honest beauty. He gets me started making a cabin that will have a dormer and a loft. The day he leaves me on my own I am scared of his trust.

Coming back to admire my progress, he gracefully leaves a hint about the wisdom of nailing in more braces. (One wall leans out a little where I was slow to take his gentle advice.)

By a genial cunning, he always makes me feel as if I am discovering everything for myself. More than that, an abounding energy flows forth from him. His childlike concentration is contagious. No wonder his students over the years have found him both endearing and empowering. He teaches as he lives – by sharing his exuberance.

By his love of life and his infinite enthusiasms, he creates an energy of delight, an adventurous confidence in the freedom of trial by error.

The Uncertain Muck

We do not stand on one leg and pray as the heron does, with terrible patience, at the sea's edge; but the same margin calls us, encircles us with a hungry claim, where we wait, expectant and persistent, ever greedy for gift.

We see ourselves also in those black ducks so near the shore, endlessly diving. For we too would probe the uncertain muck, bottom-feeding on the dark and the deep.

If neither heron nor duck share a passion for roses, or depend upon their unneccesity, their world merges with the innocence of roses. Their bushes are already hosting the black-spots, mites and rusts of time's unsolicited gifts.

All things so swiftly become the bearer of an uncertain future.

Yet our best will remains one with briar roses, blighted and wind-torn, with hunger-halted herons, and scavenger ducks searching silted depths.

We love the sensual splendour of this improvisitory and spend-easy life, lifting and falling, sweetly unpredictable, and as glad in gravity as grace.

Serene Energy

We need both rest and restlessness. We need both to fall into a deepening peace, and to stir and rise and hunt again. We need both a still centering and a clamorous vigour.

After sabbatical repose, we demand the tumult of trial and error. After a most secret brooding, we are pushed to shatter the shell and drop from the nest. Grounded for a while, we search for new bearings. We want perfect peace without loss of excitement, a tranquil freedom.

How shall we equally affirm the warm world of withdrawal and the wide world of adventure?

May the enlivening will for opposites, the alternating currents of desire, permit us soundly to sleep and gladly to wake.

Secure us in our warm nests and renew us for our dark flights.

The Will Beyond the Barrier

He is a wiry, fine boned boy. Just home from school, he sees us sitting in spring light beyond the sliding glass doors of the sun deck. He runs swiftly towards us with his widest smile, his arms stretched wide with the love which would embrace us.

Then, like a beautiful bird mistaking a course of flight, swiftly his delicate body smashes against the painful shock of closed pane of glass.

So his mother holds him in her arms, against her wildly beating breast.

If only this were all, an unlikely accident of childhood; but love's brutal impediments will reappear in ever new forms. There is an unseen wall between lover and loved, between desire and embodiment.

Yet desire is infinite. We remain hungry for love.

Without Power

Among the things we like about winter are the power-breaks that often come with wind-storms. Despite obvious inconveniences, the deprivation is an occasion to be enjoyed.

First, we become aware of an uncommon silence, without the hum of furnace motor, blower, fridge and freezer.

We lay and light a fire in the fire-place to take the place of both furnace and kitchen range. We place candles in holders about the house.

At last, snug inside, we are bathed in the light and warmth of the fireplace as the storm sweeps and rattles the house. Even Teddy senses our happiness and makes himself lap-comfortable.

Family were visiting on the night of the last "outage." We talked in the glow of the fire and flickering candles. We reminisced in intimate stillness. When Marc played the piano, we joined together singing old songs.

Suddenly the power came on with lights, furnace and fridge. Candles were snuffed with regret and resignation. Snuffed out also was a renewing remnant of sacred simplicity. We were all startled by the sense of loss, but what else could we do?

We believe in the holy catholic church of technology.

The Call of the Migratory

Walking in the prayer of this November woods, I crush the lingering red berries of the huckleberry, bright as blood, innocent emblems of an emptying. A crow cries. Yellow leaves tremble. Pale mushrooms shove up against the dark.

A stony sky weighs down on the sullen shoulders of the mountain. The birds of summer have long ago gathered and departed. The river mouth opens to striving salmon compelled to swim upstream. Eagles, crows and gulls feed on their dead bodies – those that have already spawned.

I am dizzy from standing at the edge where waters of life and death meet, caught up in the swirl of tide rolling in, river rolling out, the evening air busy with birds wheeling, sweeping by, diving again and again, stopping only to feed on their blood catch. Everything in air and water is in motion, in the vortex of all that feeds and is eaten. The sea-swollen river is both seminary and sepulchre. The beginning and the end meets here.

It helps to know this place of arrival and departure, this cycle of costly communion.

The bruised salmon's upstreaming, and our own wild hunger are captive in the same swift spending.

The Prayer of a Bare Beach

We would be as right as the rounded boulders in
dialogue with sea.

We would be as clean as the scoured driftwood,
arranged and re-arranged by meditations of moon.

We would be as still as the Great Blue Heron,
poised at the very edge, for what the tide brings in.

We would be as sure as the cycling salmon, buoyant
and brave, on the way that circles home.

From the First Laugh

Life was only made possible by the first person who laughed at it. Were it not for the laughter just east of Eden, all would have died screaming. Neither inarticulate groaning nor stupendous sobbing could have atoned for life's enthralling cruelty.

An early, unknown saint who could not take things too seriously, the first person to laugh out loud, secured our salvation, once and for all.

If only levity were contagious.

A Rite of Morning

A Kwakiutl elder tells of the days when the rising sun was greeted with a ceremony of cleansing and empowerment at the shore.

"I rose early. In the returning sun, I went down to the sea. I stripped bare. Standing at the edge, I raised my arms to the light, in thanks for the renewal of day. I waded in, immersed myself and returned to shore. I gave thanks for the renewal of my life, for the return of strength after sleep. Now I was clean and strong for the day."

They were received, they were renewed, they knew their own strength, they were their own song.

We seek the same plunge for our strength and song, the gifts of dawn, the will of each new day.

The past cannot renew us, the future is too late. The present is our shore, the moment our edge.

The singular uniqueness of each person rises from the waters of renewal.

A Bonfire of Knots

In this November light, the sea is the only shining thing. Even trees are sullen. Yet we go down to the shore for what the tide brings. The wind has gathered a harvest of tangled treasure. The stony beach is piled with a broken drift of things set loose from toil. Among the debris of logging and fishing gear, there is a curve of gunnel from a skiff, a scrap of lid from a ship's hold, and a wooden spool once for coiling hydro wire.

Where now are the solid and the durable facts of industry and commerce?

All is fractured and floating.

What of this knotted root of cedar, once the anchor of windswept limbs? It is an emblem of need for a grounded hold.

Of this drift-knot, I will make a burnt offering to kindle anew the root of my musing.

Saved from saltchuk, wind and rain, my root-fire is a smoky stay against the ruins of dream.

Yet We Will Sing

If all the world had bread, were clothed and housed and fed, there would still be a need as great – the wine of the imagination.

The poor are always with us; life is always found wanting. Nevertheless, even a broken heart must find it's song.

By the art of nevertheless, an unlikely and irrational exultation renews the benediction from the beginning.

A Voice in the Dusk

A missionary to India is addressing the "Indian" congregation. The small congregation of Kwakiutl families listens politely. The sun is going down. The church is growing dark. From a shadowy pew a familiar voice quietly interrupts. It is the voice of an elder known for his wit and wisdom.

"Excuse me, please. Would you kindly tell us first about the religion of these people in India."

The missionary confesses at once that she really doesn't know much about their religion. She explains that with so many religions and variations of them it would be impossible to know them.

The elder is now invisible in the dusk, but his voice is clear.

"You go all the way to India to teach them your religion, while you don't know theirs. What if their religion is just as good as yours . . . or better?"

Sea, Fish and Cellar Door

Celebrate the world of slow, honour the world of small. Silent ripenings, steady gatherings, the mutual roots and manifold visits of days and nights. Affirm the generous extravagance at the heart of the whole, take pleasure in the dear ambivalence of every single thing, it's appearance and disappearance.

Nothing general is real. Only the specific, the distinct blazes being. Living in respect for the flux of each epiphanous fact, for each intimate moment, we hail the energy of that indwelling which ignites the soul.

For life abounds in the love of things we call by name – water, bread, sun, wine, wind, salt, snow and rain, sea, fish and cellar door. Or rather, not in the things in themselves, dear as they are, but in the personal way such things are handled by those who respect them.

It is the way bread is taken and broken, the way wine is poured out and shared, that tells if matter matters.

The incarnating will awaits our love of embodiment.

With Other Animals

We can hardly imagine the sorrowful loss to native peoples of their close life with other creatures, a sacred affinity which we desecrated. In totem and mask, in dance and song, the communion of all creatures was affirmed, and humanity was understood only in harmony with other animals.

Human animals once lived a full, continual and close life with other animals. Such fellowship is rare today. Many know no animals but human ones. This tragic excommunication is steadily growing. The rift becomes a chasm.

In my childhood town there was a public drinking fountain. One side was for people and the other for horses. I liked it best when we drank together, and I heard them breathing, snorting and lapping water so near while I drank from the same source.

The horseless carriage fired by internal combustion not only pollutes the world but erodes communion. We will never again be so human. As we lose fellow animals, we lose our souls.

Have we lost forever our place in the holy dance of man and beast?

The Yoke is Easy

I engaged an electrician to install two more outlets in my study. Explaining to him that there was a crawl-space off the adjoining room which gave easy access to the wiring, I left him to his work. Like most of us, while his hearing was good, he was "hard of listening." So when I came home the wood panelling of the study had been ripped apart, leaving the saw's ugly scars.

An earnest man, he lacks the elegance of ease which, in another, I envy. One day, I am attempting to repair the broken clothesline, standing with an end in each hand when he finds me. We sit on the ground opposite each other while he shows me how to make a proper splice. I covet the relaxed precision of his fingers as he weaves the strands together. "The first thing," he tells me, "is to release the tension. There's an easy way of doing things and there's a hard way. Most people choose the hard way, but they could just as well have chosen the easy."

Here's to the easy way that makes ends meet.

A Carol at Midnight

His mother called him Sandy because she gave birth to him on the sandy beach at the edge of the sea. He lives up to his name as such an elemental meeting-place. The visible and the invisible worlds meet well in him. Sound and silence meet well in him. Especially when his silence becomes song.

On Christmas Eve, just before midnight, Sandy sings Silent Night in Kwakwala. He stands as still as a cedar tree, waiting for the fullness of the moment, gathering us in the meeting-point of sound and silence. When the song is over, he remains rooted in the hush, then seals his lips and nods his head by way of confirmation.

When he suddenly grins like a proud boy it is surely Christmas morning.

Brave and Clean

We welcome September's boy coming home from kindergarten, wading through puddles in new shoes, carrying crayons, treasuring a new book and a new song.

We take a picnic to the spit. Wide open to wonder, he takes delight in ducks, becomes one himself, singing over and over again, Six Little Ducks, while the lowering sun warms the mossy bank where we sit.

Here is the world of small and slow – the nearest, closest and queerest. We study together the mounds of bronzed moss, the tiny, dry flowers on hair-thin stems, the curly leaves of silver-green lichen. A black and tan caterpillar on a furry errand.

He opens his new drawing book to its first blank page, draws and colours the caterpillar in the simple strokes of his instinctive innocence.

If only we could learn as a child again, in unblotched notebooks, with a brave, clean trust in the school of surprise.

Yes, the renewable child within is pulling us towards a freedom yet untried.

Faith in Fog

Blindly we walk in labyrinth, an impenetrable dance of particles silently circling, surrounding us. Blank eyes strain, bandaged, in a moist swirl of gauze. Taunted and teased by this tenebrous halo we are finally slowed to a halt. We are softly pressed into a veiled prison of something like nothing. We are lowered inside down. We cling to a thin fibre of hope that the darkness may find us, and give a name to our losthood.

The fog comes close to whisper in our ears. The fog has much to teach us of emptiness and unlearning. The cloud of unknowing has come down to earth for us.

One day, we become content with the sequestered, the veiled, letting the equivocal be our delight. We come to honour only the elusive, the timid, the hushed – what is here, and yet not here. Baptized into fog, we die to designations, definitions, that we may dive deeper to where the hidden dwells.

The presence we sense swirls and breathes in a wet, unnameable waiting, wrapped in nothing but awe. The faith of the fogged-in frees us, and lets us be centred, entered, and rounded – for the uttermost and final weather.

His Autumn Vespers

Late in August, just at dusk, he walks the darkening garden along the tall staked vines, lifting leaves and branches, scattering the green dust pungent with promise. He holds in his hand, while still on the vine, the ripening roundness of a tomato, the sun's ingathering. From Aztec seed, an old hymn of photosynthesis.

A last slant of sun pierces the tangle to light up his face.

Intent, zealous and tender, an old man saying good-night to his tomatoes.

Finding A Home for Ourselves

We live in the boundless infinity of the universe. Within this immensity we share a galaxy; within this milky way, the world as seen from the moon. Drawing the circle closer, we share the difficult and beguiling intimacy of others, our most familiar realm. Here, if grace prevails we may shape our most private sphere.

Nourished by the outermost and the innermost, the potential of self emerges like an island in the sea, our personal island bounded by the shores of our mortality.

One with the widest and closest of concentric worlds, we may rove full circle finding home within home – all beyond us, within, and all within us, beyond.

Tidal Pools

In some places along the shore the lay of the land lets the tide gather in limpid, dark pools teeming with life.

Seaweeds, red, green or brown, barnacles, mussels, limpets, tiny crabs, strange worms and more, much more live together in a visible and invisible colony belonging both to land and sea.

When the storms are fierce and the tides high, the morning discloses visiting creatures, purple star fish and sea urchins, moon whelk, and things I don't know.

These delicate, ever changing pools cherish and protect precarious lives as in a chalice.

I kneel in wonder, musing upon the treasure of such a dwelling place, a momentary meeting so like the unlikely mix which occasioned our beginning.

My own wavering reflection suddenly appears among the weeds and shells.

I am glad to be caught in such a holding place.

To Hold Awhile

One pale leaf falling into the dark stream. One white gull wheeling and diving down. One first star in the deepening.

One person as close as your own breathing in the sensuous thrust of intimacy.

We yield like seeds falling to earth, rain sinking into soil. We learn an autumnal acquiescence by a holding . . . and a letting go. . . .

So take in your hands the face of a flower. Take in your hands the curve of a cup. Hold in your hands the face of your love.

Hold what you may not hold for long.